PS

I DON

Chrissie Hill, Lon and short and two in 2002. Her ...ous children's poetry ...n *Now You See Me, Now You* ...was shortlisted for the first CLPE Poetry Award in 2003. She is a member of the Poetry Society's *poetryclass* training team for teachers and has been resident writer with Belmarsh Prison, the Refugee Council, Maidstone Borough Council, twelve Southwark primary schools and Croydon Libraries. She has read her children's poems at the Aldeburgh Poetry Festival, the Children's Bookshow and the Poets House in New York. In autumn 2005 Chrissie toured ten schools on the western seaboard of the Highlands, including one which she reached by boat and quad bike! www.chrissiegittins.co.uk

Kev Adamson studied at Menai College and Liverpool School of Art and Design. He works as an illustrator, animator and graphic designer; he is also an award winning website designer. Kev lives in Conwy in North Wales. www.kevadamson.com

First published in 2006
by Rabbit Hole publications
24 Elsinore Road, London SE23 2SL
Designed by LOUP
Printed by Dexters, Dartford
All rights reserved
Copyright © Text Chrissie Gittins, 2006
Copyright © Illustrations Kev Adamson, 2006
ISBN 0-9543288-1-7
978-0-9543288-1-8

Some of the poems in this book have been published in:
Velocity, The Best of Apples and Snakes (Black Spring Press, 2003)
The Poetry Store (Hodder Wayland, 2005)
The Works 4 (Macmillan, 2005)
Man in the Moon website (2005)
Best Friends (Macmillan, 2006)
The Works for Key Stage 1 (Macmillan, 2006)
Dinosaur Poems (Scholastic, 2006)
Christmas Poems (Macmillan 2006)

I DON'T WANT AN AVOCADO FOR AN UNCLE

POEMS BY CHRISSIE GITTINS

ILLUSTRATIONS BY KEV ADAMSON

Rabbit Hole Publications

By the same author

poetry for children
The Listening Station
Now You See Me, Now You …

poetry for adults
A Path of Rice
Pilot
Armature

radio drama
Poles Apart
Starved for Love
Life Assurance
Dinner in the Iguanodon

as editor
Somebody Said That Word
Thoughts in Corners

CONTENTS

For my dear family, and my dear friends

I DON'T WANT AN AVOCADO
FOR AN UNCLE

I don't want an icicle for an auntie,
she might snap.

I don't want a tomato for an older brother,
he might go red in the face.

I don't want a candle for a gran,
she might melt.

I don't want a coffee bean for a cousin,
he might get swallowed from a cup.

I don't want a blister for a sister,
she might get sore.

I don't want an avocado for an uncle,
he might go squishy.

I don't want a carpet for a granddad,
he might be threadbare.

I don't want a plum for a mum,
she might get made into chutney.

I don't want a diamond for a dad
because he'd be the hardest man in the world.

THE CAT THAT COULDN'T PURR

We had a cat that
couldn't purr.

He tried, but it came out
all in a blur.

Instead he blew wet raspberries,
as it were.

But his miaow was something
to die for.

ON THE A831, STRATHGLASS, SCOTLAND

I'm seeing a toad across the road,
he doesn't seem to know his Green Cross Code,
nor can he see the lorry coming.

So, with a soothing voice and a bit of a goad,
I'm seeing this toad across the road.

In fits and starts he tackles the tarmac.
He doesn't see the sports car's red,
the way it swerved, the way it sped,

he doesn't see the juddering juggernaut,
because he's looking dead straight ahead.

A bicycle comes and slows right down,
lets us pass, we walk around.

Then all of a sudden, without a sound,
the toad has gone –
into a hedge he's found!

A MEMORY OF SNOW
for Esther

That night the gale tilted the foreshore,
   wide rain spat at the hills,
      you turned in your thin deep bed,
        asleep with staring eyes.

      As snow rose up the mountains,
    scree on peaks washed through,
  you dreamt of herons on goatherds,
of the way a buzzard flew.

You woke to six bare mountains,
   to one with a memory of snow,
      to sheep climbing the staircase,
        to blink at a face they know.

     A stag came into the garden,
   he bowed his head to the ground,
  dislodged his rack of antlers –
his gift for you to find.

WHAT DO YOU SUPPOSE?

If I get up in the morning
and find a shoe on the lawn,
a shoe on the patio,
a sandal in a flower pot –
what do you suppose?

If I take them inside
and find another shoe is missing
and I find that shoe
upside-down in a freshly dug hole –
what do you suppose?

That I left the back door open by mistake?
That while I was sleeping a fox crept in?
That she giggled loudly as she passed my door?

Did she peep at me sleeping?
Did she hear my sonorous snore?

WARREN RABBIT
for my brother Warren!

Warren Rabbit has whiskers,
Warren Rabbit has sideburns,
Warren Rabbit can be jolly,
Warren Rabbit can be stern.

Warren Rabbit eats Swiss chocolates,
Warren Rabbit wears a sporran,
Warren Rabbit builds strong bridges,
Warren Rabbit sings in his warren.

THE TWO-TOED SLOTH'S BOAST

I may be a two-toed sloth,
but you should see me move,
I can run faster than a garden snail,
though I do not like to boast.

I go to the toilet once a week,
I never need a drink,
I suck the moisture from my food –
it leaves me time to think.

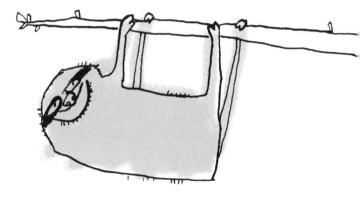

RIVER TORRIDGE

I knew the river hid
behind the bank,
lying, like a length of silk,
stretched between the willows.

The surface ripped,
something dived –
gone too long to be a bird.

Weasel head above the water,
down he went again,
a flash of oily fur.

He swam up beside,
this time he stayed,
looking at me straight.
I walked to keep his pace.

I loved his length –
his tail his body,
his body his tail,
his tail the river's length.
We moved together
through the wind,
along the river's course.

Another dive,
I skimmed the current,
searching for his guise.

He'd gone on alone.
I felt him though,
gliding through
the river's strength.

ZOO SCAR

The penguins saw it –
they all stood by
when I slipped on the mud
and bashed in my eye
on the railings.

The penguins saw it –
put their wings to their beaks,
"There's blood dripping," they said,
"that'll take weeks
to heal."

The penguins saw it –
but it's all right now.
I've a scar to show,
a story to tell,
and a little nick
over my left eyebrow.

FLAMINGO BLUMINGO

Flamingos are gregarious birds,
they rarely stand alone,
twenty thousand in one place,
not one allowed to moan.

For if they started –
"My leg is aching,"
"A bone's stuck in my U-bend neck,"
they'd drive each other flamingo crazy,
so they just say, "Flipping heck!"

LIMERICK 1

There was a young boy from Peru,
who never knew quite what to do.
He rubbed his nose
and wriggled his toes,
then painted his village bright blue.

THE NIGHT FLIGHT OF
THE PTERODACTYL

As I wait for the right current of air
a moonbeam glistens on my claw.

I take off from the highest mountain –
not without grace,
not without speed,
and with a spine of pride
which tingles to my gleaming teeth –
I'm the largest creature to fly.

Gliding over the lake I make
a black shadow with my shape,
warm blood pumps through my jaw.

I swoop on a sleeping frog,
look up at the swarming stars,
then end his dream with a snap.

NESSIE'S ADVICE

Most folk think there's only me,
but I've an extended family –
an auntie and a wife,
when we gather in the fathoms
the gossiping is rife.

In turn we break the surface –
maybe once a year,
to titillate the tourists,
emit a ripple of fear.

We're plesiosaurs, of course we are,
and to all those who camp
and peer across the loch,
with binoculars and telescopes,
nips, and flasks of soup,

we beg of you,
before this century's out –
go somewhere warmer,
and please, get a life.

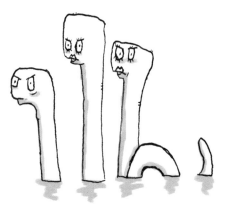

ICH-ICHTHYOSAUR

I'm lithe on the land,
I'm fast in the sea,
not a fish, or a lizard –
though my name means both,
no, I'm me!

I'm a Flat-toothed Ich,
while my friend is Slender-snouted,
and we're never apart for long.

We avoid Common Ichs,
for they do have a penchant –
especially on a Tuesday,
to pong.

We like best of all
to sunbathe on sand,
with a mermaid's purse on each eye.

When the sun goes down
we lollop up the shore,
then slide in the sea with a sigh.

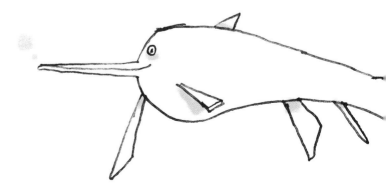

IGOR IGUANODON

I may weigh four and a half tons,
but I like to think
when it comes to food
I have a little finesse.

I fill up on cycads and zamia,
then my absolute favourite
is bluebells and clover
followed by a dish of vetch and woad.

I go a long way for foxgloves,
even further for spurge,
when I've a yen for an orchid –
nothing satisfies the urge
but a pool of purple in June.

My herd think I'm mad,
but when I breathe in the perfume
and savour the flavours
I really couldn't give a tad.

LIMERICK 2

There was a young girl from Dunoon,
who ate heather honey from a spoon,
it made her real sweet,
put a spring in her feet,
now each week she leaps over the moon.

WHEN IS A BOY NOT A BOY?
for Oswald and Selhurst Boys

When is a boy not a boy?
When he's a plank of wood.

When is a boy a plank of wood?
When he goes rigid with fear.

When does a boy go rigid with fear?
When he's being carried across the river.

When is a boy carried across the river?
When he's the smallest in a party of boys
being chased by bullocks.

When is a boy part of a party of boys
being chased by bullocks?
When they're being taken for a walk
to the nearest village by their history teacher.

When is a boy taken for a walk
to the nearest village by his history teacher?
When he's staying in a thatched farmhouse
to do creative writing in the middle of Devon.

When does a boy stay in a thatched farmhouse
to do creative writing in the middle of Devon?
When he's capable of becoming a plank of wood.

THE BALLET TEACHER

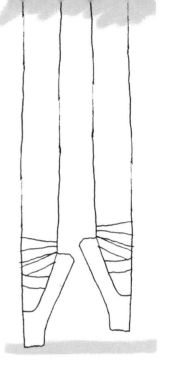

She walks on a bottomless duvet,
her arms carve arcs in the air –

fingers outstretched,
boat-bottom hands,

they fall like feathers
never reaching the ground.

Her circle skirt pleats
glide behind her, beside her,

folding, unfolding –
an opening fan.

Her voice glances each child
with gossamer.

QUEENS
for Tess

One day, while out walking,
the Queen Of Asking Stupid Questions met
the Queen Of Stating The Obvious.
"Are you walking to Town?"
asked the Queen Of Asking.
"This is such a long road,"
said the Queen Of Stating,
peering at the spires in the distance.
The sky was purple and grey.

"Will it rain, do you think?"
asked the Queen Of Asking.
"This umbrella is full of holes,"
said the Queen of Stating.
Her curls dripped down her cheeks.

"Will it take long?" asked Asking.
"As long as it takes," said Stating.

MR FOGG THE VERY
FRIENDLY DENTIST

Mr Fogg's a dentist
who explains as he goes along,
that while my mouth is frozen,
I must not bite my tongue.

There's a humongous needle
aiming at my mouth,
"Apologies," says my dentist
as it lodges beside my tooth.

My chin goes numb, I can't feel a thing,
the drill comes inside,
the motorway construction starts,
"That's right, keep opening wide."

"I'm nearly there, just a bit to go,
this tooth's in an awkward place.
There we are, I've got it all,
 now you can relax your face."

The amalgam squeaks inside my tooth,
the job is almost done,
rinse out, chair up, pick up my coat,
this visit was almost fun!

MASTER DO-JUST-BUT-HAVE-TO

As he leaves the house George says,
"Oh I do-just-but-have-to get a packet of Hoola-hoops
from the kitchen."

As he gets on the bus he says,
"Oh I do-just-but-have-to buy a copy of that
new computer magazine."

As he gets out his bus fare he says,
"Oh I do-just-but -have-to count all the money
in my trouser pockets to make sure
I've got enough for dinner."

As he walks in class he says,
"Oh I do-just-but-have-to collect my home-work
from my friends who have been, well not really copying,
just getting ideas when we were on the bus."

As the teacher calls out his name he says,
"Oh I do-just-but-have-to find that book
I was looking for yesterday in the library."

As he walks into his first lesson of the day he says,
"Oh I do-just-but-do-have-to remember to look as if I'm
concentrating on what the teacher is saying otherwise
she will get very cross."

MY GRANDMA IS A NUN

My Grandma picks the blackberries,
the plums and apples too,
she feeds the ducks
and feeds the hens,
she sees the morning dew
before she goes to say the prayers
for me, and you, and you.

She writes on her computer,
she reads great big thick books,
she makes the jam and chutney
and helps out other cooks.

At weekend she plans the menu,
picks parsley, chives and thyme,
my Grandma is a fun nun,
and apart from God's, she's mine.

THREE

My best friend *has* a best friend,
she is a bester friend than me,
but when they have a falling out
my friend is best with me.

LIFELINE

Your clothes still smell of cinnamon and garlic,
your hand of lavender and musk,

despite the drenching and the soaking,
the days you must have floated

between stern and sodden deck.
Chesil's arm of sand beckoned,

guided you to Wyke,
and here you lie, who are you?

with stained glass blue all round you
bringing your dead eyes alight.

You've knotted wrack and thong-weed
plaited through your hair,

I'll pick it out and keep it,
lay these lilies at your feet,

bring flowers to you daily,
be your sister while you need me,

sweep the aisle, wipe the altar,
I'll see you claimed, all right.

Your lips are grey as lias,
your fingers hold the air,

your bones are made from beauty,
when I touch your arm, you care.

Mary Anning (palaeontologist
and fossil hunter) visited the
body of a woman washed
ashore in 1815 after the
Alexander sailing ship was
wrecked off the Dorset coast.

CHERUB BOB WAS A SLOB

Cherub Bob was a slob,
he wiped his nose
on his sleeve.
He left his feathers out
in all kinds of weathers,
till they got a horrid disease.

Now Bob is more careful,
he uses cloud tissue,
and spreads his wings
under trees, to dry in the sun
and when he has done,
he jumps off his golden trapeze.

LIMERICK 3

There was a young man from Bulgaria,
who feared persistent malaria,
"Get off me you flea",
he said, hitting his knee,
the mosquito is by far the more scarier.

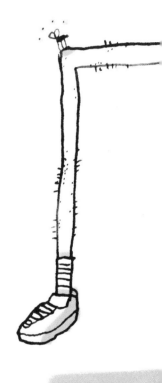

FIGURE

When I arrived Suilven
wore a scarf of cloud

across her shoulder.
Next day, pouting at Canisp,

a chestnut beret at half cock.
Her skirts were low

with mist on Thursday.
Today, her shape,

with sun, is kissed.

Suilven and Canisp are mountains
in the Highlands of Scotland.

NYNY

Beware,
I
have
New York
in my eyes.
Balconies with a
closed lid of snow,
two poached eggs in
a cup, the flash of
static as my finger
hits the Chrysler tower.
A lift flying eighty
floors in less than
a minute, a lift
which never comes,
an unflushable toilet,
a toilet which
flushes when I open
the door. A window
from my room looks
into an opposite room –
a woman wears
antennae to watch
TV. A tall man with
wide Halloween hair,
black lenses in his
eyes, bends low to
kiss his small pale
girlfriend on the
forehead. The snow
is stacked in mountain
ranges at the end of
each sidewalk.
Care is needed to get
across to the other side.

BENCHES, TRESCO

They're placed at considerate intervals –
curved hurricane pine,
some weathered and scored,

some lichened and worn,
some with holes –
where the trunk swallowed a branch.

From a bench I saw a blackbird with an orange beak,
the promise of protea in fat downy buds,
the chequerboard bark of an endless palm.

From a bench I saw wagtails surrounding a horse,
the stripes of shelduck tipped up in a lake,
the oblique flight of pheasants.

From a bench I saw Atlantic waves
drawing breath, raising their shoulders
and spewing their seething froth right back to the shore.

From a bench I saw an insect in flight,
the blades of its wings whirred away from the island,
it carried me back to rumbling ground.

WORLD SECRETS

The people of Hungary have huge appetites,
Romania has no space at all,
Newfoundland has yet to be discovered,
In Trinidad the fathers have a ball.

You won't find a telegraph wire in Poland,
Armenia is full of generous souls,
In Russia the men walk slowly,
The houses in Andorra don't have doors.

In Finland no one eats fish,
Minnows are eaten by Wales,
In Turkey they prefer chicken,
In Sardinia, a piece of toast never fails.

In Germany all children are squeaky clean,
In Greece they cook with olive oil,
In Cuba the people are very round,
Iceland is a country always on the boil.

Chile is the place for jumpers,
In Korea everyone gets ahead,
In Jersey they wear cardigans,
In Kuwait they've given up

and
    gone
        home
           to
              bed.

LIMERICK 4

There was a young man from Capri,
who had a very sore knee,
he slathered it in balm
and ruptured his arm,
and ran home to drink cups of tea.

(with sugar)

WISH SANDWICH

Between two slices of
the Caspian Sea
I'd like a yellow lilo

Inside a
crunchy cedar bun
I'd like high season
in the sun

Call it a wrap
with a whale
inside and
clouds of
minnows
on the
side

Last
of all I'd like
a roll with a feather
filling for my
soul

PICCALILLI AND BOTTLE TOP

Piccalilli is a yellow child
with an onion for her head.
Her legs are stalks of cauliflower,
she lies on a mustard bed.

You can't mistake Bottle Top,
for whenever he is near,
a distinctive rattle, clink-clonk-click
is all that you will hear.

Bottle Top and Piccalilli
are truly best of friends.
If he rattles on, or she gets too sour,
they always make amends.

One day they went to the seaside,
a man spotted Lill on the sands,
he shoved her inside his sandwich
with his great big pork pie hands.

B.T. was quick into action,
he danced on Pork Pie's head,
his eyes rolled around at the awful sound
and his face went Ribeena red.

Lill slipped away to the ocean,
Bottle Top was soon on her tail,
they had a very nice day at Westgate Bay –
Pork Pie was squashed by a whale.

LIMPET

I am a Cornish limpet,
  been here for a hundred years,
    sucking and gripping and sticking to this stone
      with a hundred thousand fears.

        What if I get put in a bucket
          and dumped in the boot of a car,
            with wellies and jellies and a windbreaker
              and a shell in the shape of a star?

            I'd miss my chats with the ancient crab,
              the swell and wash of the tide,
                the soothing stroke of anemones,
                  the storms when the fish come and hide.

                But I hang on tight and hope for the best,
                  I avoid anyone with a spade,
                    when the sun beats down in a glisten
                      on the sea, my fears begin to fade.

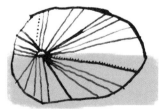

THE POINTLESSNESS OF NOT BUYING YOUR OWN STRAWBERRY ICE CREAM

"Can I have a lick?"
"No."

"Can I have a bite?"
"No."

"Can I have the end with
a bit of ice-cream on it?"
"No."

"Well can I have a lick then?"
"No!"

RIDDLE

It's a boat in the air,
it swings and it rocks.
it carries a pair of glasses,
two books, a pair of holey socks.

It's stripy and it's dappled,
it lies in dark and shade,
it's a place to float away,
to forget the existence of clocks.

The answer to this riddle is
somewhere in this book!

WETSUIT MAN

There was a man from Ullapool,
who jumped off the pier in his wetsuit.

It made a change from sorting his change,
And he learned his left from his right foot.

MAKING DAISY CHAINS

While we are making daisy chains
a man is having a jog,

While we are making daisy chains
a toddler leans over a log,

While we are making daisy chains
a wasp is chased by a dog,

While we are making daisy chains
a couple is having a snog.

LIMERICK 5

There was a young woman from Nantucket,
who lived all her life in a bucket,
in an aim to break free,
and live in a tree,
she climbed up a rowan to suck it
and see.

HOW TO MAKE A CUP OF TEA
for William Patten School, Stoke Newington

Take the mouse out of the teapot.
Pour in two cupfuls of ice.

Boil the kettle and leave the water to cool.
Find some tea.
This could be elephant and magnet tea,
hundreds and thousands tea,
or – the always popular – bag of nails tea.

Shovel the tea into the pot.
Don't bother pouring out the iced water –
it will mingle nicely with the cool water
from the kettle.
Pour the water from the kettle steadily
into the teapot. Leave it for half an hour
to settle down and stop giggling.

Find six teacups. Six is always a good number.
Don't worry about the saucers.
Never make the mistake of asking
if anyone takes sugar.
If they say 'Yes' and you've run out,
then you'll have to go out and buy some.

Milk the cat.
Bake a cake.

THE PENCIL STUB
again for William Patten School

When I was new I drew
the leather shoe lace on a magic shoe.

You shaved me down.

I wound my lead around
the leaves of an ancient
willow tree.

You shaved me down.

I drew a circle, you
rubbed me out,
I became a careful square.

You shaved me down.

I was happiest tracing
the face of your mother –
her plaited hair,
her sparkling slate grey eyes.

And still you shaved me down.

I could still conjure the universe,
skirt Saturn with a silver ring,
chase the rain falling from
a shooting star.

WALTER THE WATER WIZARD

If you have a headache
I swim up the tap
and add a little aspirin
to give that pain a zap.

When you're in the shower
and you run out of gel,
I wriggle up the showerhead
and squirt a dreamy smell.

If you're in the swimming pool
convinced you're going to sink,
I'm standing underneath you –
floating's easier than you think.

My favourite though is making snow
from the dampness in the sky,
every flake is different –
they land on your hand with a sigh.

YELLOW FAIRY
(MOBILE NUMBER 0999099909990)

A fairy is as a fairy does
and what I do is wrinkles.
If a fairy frowns

and furrows her brow
I remove the lines
with a scoop.

Then I store them in boxes
in a thick tree trunk
and keep them dry till the Spring.

When the primrose grows
with its smooth smooth leaves,
the rain beats them to a ruin –

so I carry my frowns far into the wood
and set to work with speed,
pressing wrinkle after wrinkle in the leaves.

Then, the rain runs down
the wrinkled leaves,
and the flowers bloom butter on the floor.

So if you do have a wrinkle
please give me a call –
for I'm always wanting more.

TEDDY BALLOON

I blew up my balloon with helium
and let go of the string.
It flew above my garden,
bob-bobbing in the wind.

It flew above the houses,
above a chimney pot,
it flew along with seagulls
till it was a tiny dot.

It cleared the misty mountains,
dissolved into a cloud,
"Come back, my bouncy Teddy,
Come back," I cried out loud.

But Teddy's gone forever,
away over the sea.
Now I know, I can cry,
but he won't come back to me.

FLANNEL, SOAP, COMB

Flannel soft, flannel fleecy,
wipe across your face.
Take away the dribbles
running in a race –
down your chin.

Soap, to make a lather,
slides across your cheeks.
Rub it hard with water,
bubbles stand in peaks –
on your nose.

Comb, to smooth the tangles,
pull it through your hair.
Drag it hard and you will
hooooowwwwllllll, like a bear –
in *(choose)* Mummy's ear.
         Daddy's

GOING TO BE LATE FOR SCHOOL

It's hard to walk fast in the morning
when there's a washing machine
in my tummy.

It churns and swirls my toast and jam,
while I jump
the cracks in the pavement.

Three more turnings to go –
my tea is rinsing my Frosties.

Mums and Dads walk towards me,
the lollipop lady has gone.

I launch into a flat spin,
hang up my coat,

race to my classroom –
the register has just begun.

LIMERICK 6

There was a young girl from Havant,
who walked with a bit of a slant,
"You have got a lean,"
said her friend Billy-Jean,
so she applied for an angle transplant.

THE YEAR IS TURNING

Gulls chance the churning sea,
    Leaves stack up against the thermal door,
Tips of willows, russet, finger low grey sky.
    The year is drawing in.

Old man's beard billows by the road,
    A net of mist hangs over Swanbourne Lake,
Rosehips thrust from scratchy hedgerows.
    The year is turning in.

TIN LID

Underneath the bedclothes late at night
I read by the light of a torch –

no give away crack that way
of light from my bedroom door.

If the battery was flat I'd chance my arm
with an old tin lid from a jam pot.

Stealing birthday candles
from the kitchen drawer

I'd melt each end on the lid.
Under the covers, the candles lit,

I read my books at this altar.
The thing set alight was my mind.

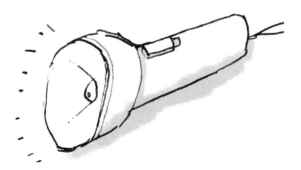

MY EARS HAVE SPOKEN

Think of your ears at the side of your head,
think of your ears above your mouth,
each time your lips utter a word
your ears surround the sound –

like stereo speakers
they pick up the beat
of every single word you speak.

Write down the words, as they're said,
but how do we know they are spoken?
Around the words are four tiny ears –
inverted commas they're known as.

BRANDED

If you buy a Coke from Tesco
followed by a Beano and a Twix,
then add Cheerios to your basket
and a box of Weetabix,

If you make a phone call on a Nokia,
play Nintendo while you eat
a Wall's ice cream which dribbles down
the Nikes on your feet,

If you feed your cat on Friskies
and crunch on Walkers crisps,
wear glasses from Spec Savers,
use Sony computer disks,

Then you'll need a stack of CAPITALS
for the start of each word which
stands for a brand name –
each one you've ever heard.

STORING TIME

*(In answer to the question 'What happens
to time after it is spent?')*

All last year's nights
are in black bags
at Euston.

Paddington houses Lost Time
in rows of sieves
beyond Lost Property.

Bright sparkling mornings
are in clear plastic pockets
lining each horizon.

Birthdays are the grains
of gunpowder cracking fire
from Roman Candles.

Moments of supreme happiness
are held in bubbles
rising from the mouths of guppies.

Sadness lives in cinders
waiting to be steamrollered
beneath the road.

Each and every
touch and hug and kiss and smile and sneeze,
is dancing with the dragonflies, up and down the breeze.

PUTTING AWAY CHRISTMAS

The cards sit in a pile – a child,
dressed as a Christmas pudding,
walks along the top.

The tree lies outside –
pointing the way
for a council collection.

The fairy lights are curled up
inside their plastic box,
resting their filaments for another year.

Time to fold gold wrapping into bags,
read instructions on presents,
press my finger

on the last crumbs
of the Christmas cake,
and lick the sweetness away.

hammock